SHALL WE GATHER
AT THE RIVER?

Shall We Gather at the River?

IRENE RAWNSLEY

LITTLEWOOD

Poems © Irene Rawnsley 1990
Cover Design © Kate Rawnsley
Published by Littlewood + Arc, The Nanholme Centre,
Todmorden, Lancashire OL14 6DA
Printed by Arc & Throstle Press, Todmorden
Typeset by Anne Lister Typesetting, Halifax

ISBN: 0 946407 51 1

Acknowledgements are due to 'Northern Poetry One', where five of
these poems appeared alongside others by prizewinners in the
First Northern Poetry Competition held in 1989.

CONTENTS

TWO CHAIRS AND A CANDLE

There was dry rot
in our basement flat;
you recognized the smell
having been a woodwork student.
We had a workbench in the kitchen;

no other furniture to start with
except two chairs
left by the previous tenants.
We sat on these by candlelight
until the electric was fixed.

You sold your trumpet
to buy wood and made
a bed, table, two easy chairs
though none of them
was ever completely finished.

Our baby was born in the new bed.
You cooked black toast,
coaxed the water heater into action,
bought flowers, refused
to wash her nappies.

Upstairs a husband beat his wife;
She asked us to keep
tins of silver coins
and a cardboard box of letters
which might be used in evidence.

One day the wife pushed a note
under our door;
I feared infection from her misery,
pleaded to move.
You found us another place.

KATY DATA
For my daughter

Birth of a girl child; Sunday,
All Saints Day, twenty minutes to midnight,
in a rented bedroom.
Hair, black. Face, imperious.
The grandiose marble fireplace
flame-lit with logs comes into its own
one final time. Rotting lino hesitates.
Call this child Kathleen.
She'll hate the name; at six answer to Katy,
at fifteen seek the dignity of Kate.

'Worse than any lad!'
The breadman removes his cap
before this tiny destroying angel.
Other children's toys, taken apart
with loving attention.
Two years, three years on
those same experimental fingers
shape a world of paper birds, necklaces, dolls;
on my birthday
a bead embroidered pencil case, YMMUM.

Respectable as statues
on the stone seat of the patio,
Kate with Andrew, her first boyfriend,
clutching his Fleetwood Mac L.P.
Later comes Dr. Who in ankle-length scarf,
Medallion Man, a rocker in dragon denims.
She chooses none of them,
prefers collecting old bottles,
plays the clarinet, cricket in the street,
cycles to distant bird reserves,

draws passionately, paints, prints,
pits herself against life's odds
to sort it her way, won't be
a caught, contented housewife.
She attends the mirror of her art,
affirms its joy through heart's affairs,
financial crises, chasms of self-doubt,
insecurities, bewilderments.
Kathleen, Katy, Kate,
you've welcomed your own woman.

8

FANNY TRUELOVE

Miss Truelove showed me her wedding dress one day,
cream cotton and sepia lace wrapped in tissue,
kept underneath sheets in the linen box by her bed.
Edward was silver-framed in the sideboard drawer;
he'd left for America from their Oxfordshire village,
returned after ten years with a wife and little girl.
Nothing changed for Fanny. She continued to run
the family bakery, saw brother George married
but none of her sisters; all went single to the grave,
she at eighty-four the last one left.
She cradled my baby daughter in tough old arms,
opened her heart and house to us both.
Her days were full of treasures she unwrapped
from cocoons of newspaper to handle at the fireside;
nine apostle spoons, half a shell-china tea set,
embroidered cloths, shawls, a string of amber beads.
'These was Anne's, poor Anne. She never took to moving,
never wore her things, lost mother's brooches;
I wonder what went of them? Annie blamed
the men they sent from Pickfords.' This catalogue
of missing articles grew with time. A soup ladle,
old photographs, hats, Japanese silk pictures,
crochet gloves; 'I wonder what went of them?'
Smoothing of papers, long staring into the fire.
'I suppose they was in the box the men took.'

ARTIST IN RESIDENCE

I never realized
how special was your gift
until you started to bring home
paintings from your Art class.

Always the figures echoed yourself,
short solid men,
backs to the outside world,
gazing at a harbour thronged with boats.

The colours were sombre;
sulphur, slate-grey, sullen red;
nothing to lure the eye
into open sea space.

Yet I liked them,
propped them round the room for company,
used a picture one day
to block the grate,
coaxing alight a sulky fire.
You were due home in half an hour;
pans were bubbling over in the kitchen.

Such flames when I returned!
The oils burned daring colours;
blue tropical seas,
green luminous fish,
purple fireflies.
Even as I stuffed them up the chimney
I admired the display.

You were furious,
couldn't believe my carelessness,
began at once a bigger version,
more men contemplating boats.
This time I understood those lowering hues,
could sense electric energy
stored in the colours, waiting for release.

BLAKE AND BETJEMAN

As a child my taste in poetry was extreme;
I liked Ella Wheeler Wilcox and Kipling,
knew 'The Kingdom of Love' by heart,
recited chunks of 'Hanging Danny Deevers'.

In adolescence I learned the poetry of God,
Proverbs and Psalms, Ecclesiastes,
Revelations, Song of Solomon,
with C.S. Lewis to explain the text.

The Bible wasn't good for me,
nurtured old guilts and fathered new ones;
I lost its beauty beneath a plethora of mores,
took to reading Betjeman and Blake.

Here was comfort. John Betjeman seemed
someone who believed and didn't believe,
who prayed to God and blamed Him; kept faith
against the clarity of opposing evidence.

I wore his lines on my thoughts like gloves,
felt at home with the living-room language,
quiet humour, affectionate understanding
of what it means to be human.

Blake, on the other hand, terrified me
with the awesomeness of life and God.
I read 'Hear the voice of the Bard!'
like an electric message, hot from space;

'Songs of Experience' became a touchstone
for my tangled attempts to fathom love.
The poems lit love's cruelty and pain,
scorched the skin from fake morality.

I copied them both; wrote Blake pastiches
in my frightened moods, Betjeman hymns
to fortify my calms; these two became
close to me as friends or lovers,

stand on my shelf today with later loves;
Larkin, Robert Frost, John Clare,
Emily Dickinson, Heaney, Christopher Smart,
Hardy, George Herbert, Stevie Smith.

GOING UNDERGROUND

Pen, books, papers in an oval basket
were kept on a shelf away from children.
Only after bedtime was it lifted down.
I didn't write much in those days;
articles, a few unpublished poems,
but it seemed important to try.
So much of my own sweet life went
underground in the cause of being mother.
If I switched on the radio
fingers fiddled with the knobs for 'mookits'.
Reading, they sat toys on my book,
poked holes through the newspaper,
pulled stitches from my mindless knitting.
It seemed best to give myself;
I sang songs they liked, told nursery rhymes,
read favourite stories to the point of madness,
fostered artistic gifts with paint and paper.
Absorbed by these new demanding loves
I feared the withering of other things
I cared about; words, music, books,
but found when time came round
the streams still flowing, liquid as ever
under the fretful years of motherly living.

BLUEPRINTS

For Peter

One son,
born in November
had a passion for drawing
what he called 'Guy Fawkes',
thin men stretched
longer every day as if
on a rack of pain;
from margins of books
they grew to his own height
on the wall
and longer;
when his art outreached himself
he drew on newspapers,
glued pieces together;
we walked on tortured victims
in the hall.

He grew to like speed
and danger,
reeled his long shadow
over motorcycling miles
and when roads weren't long enough
took to the air;
now hangs upon thermals,
coaxes the wind to deliver
his stork's-eye view
of linear distances.

OUT

I've been out today,
pushing my ark of children
past the Church of the Venerable Bede
to buy beans and bones for tea.
I burned the lot while rocking the baby.

You woke him up, shouting.
Don't you care how it makes him cry?
A child's too young to see trouble.

Out. The door slammed.
Jimmy Shand playing on the wireless.
We danced, my children and me,
the baby laughing, wanting to join in;
I danced him in my arms

until the nappies boiled over,
soapy rivers under the door,
one of the cork tiles raised.

You came home too soon;
I was meaning
to mop up the mess.

Time to put my dreams to sleep
lying with you in the iroko bed
you made for us.
Such clever hands.
You can make anything.
But you won't make a wife out of me.

CALLERS

There were men in my life
during my housebound years,
I have to admit it.
There was the milkman
who told stories of the doings
on the council estate;

Once he'd seen a tormented woman
trying to do her washing
in a leaky twin-tub;
she had water running in from the tap,
was sweeping the flood
from the back door with a broom.

Most days came Mr. Bateson
with his vegetable van,
sly, patient, full of innuendo.
'You can't resist my tomatoes?
I like a weak-willed woman.'
How we all shrieked!

Mondays, Wednesdays, Fridays
came the breadman
who so admired my little daughter,
and once a week the dustbin men
who invited her (she was delighted)
to the Bramley Dustbin Dance.

Thursday afternoons, but fortnightly
the door would open
to a head in a blue peaked cap;
'Pop man, love!'
Then one day, since I bought no lemonade,
'Do you get your pop off us?'

Tea-time brought my own man,
breadwinner, island of conversation,
daddy to the children,
master in his own house,
'This place is like a pig bin',
sparing us two hours from his busy schedule.

LOVE GIFTS

She hated the handbag Robert bought for her birthday,
stuffed its square black shape back into wrappers
after she'd shown it; 'like a doctor's bag';
preferred her worn brown leather shopper,
useful for carrying gifts. Millie was an artist in giving.
My childhood Christmases were warm with picture books,
fancy dolls, red velvet dreses, chocolate novelties.
For starting Grammar School she gave a hockey bag,
a dynamo when I rode a bike, Max Factor when thirteen,
cut glass for my engagement, expensive linen to set up home.
Robert died; she couldn't drive but still came visiting,
complained of standing in the cold at bus stops,
her bag full of gifts for my children; sweets, wax crayons,
puzzles, pretty dresses, furry slippers.

One Easter came a phone call. Millie had died at a bus stop;
most of her valuables were in the bag she carried,
purse, papers, building society book and a small bone box
containing a sapphire ring. Her will confirmed
this was for me, a last bequest. I wear it sometimes,
watch the cold stones flash but it's an empty pleasure.
The joy of her gifts lay in the love that lived in them.
Did she guess this? I wish I'd found a way to tell her so.

GIRLFRIENDS

You brought the first one to church.
She spent a cheerful hour and a half
unwrapping mintoes and
adjusting her hearing aid;
it whistled during the sermon.

Alice brought Clarry,
arthritic and full of demands.
She needed an armchair
set in the aisle;
those wooden pews didn't do for her hip.

Florrie liked cider vinegar;
we spent an afternoon
scouring the shops for it.
She drank two bottles a week but
still was miserable.

You bought a Volvo
to get them all in;
it took several hours on Sundays,
stage-managing their sticks and pills,
whether to wear this hat, a warmer coat.

I tried to help,
sewed an acreage of curtains
to keep out the draught for Marjorie
who had style but no money,
bought seedless grapes

for blind Mrs. Ritson.
You looked at me with horror;
'You can't have forgotten,
she died last month.'
I knew then I'd have to leave.
The competition was becoming too great.

S * X

It was the dirtiest,
most interesting of sins,
brought more froth to the corners
of the mouths of urgent preachers
than all the other six.

Even in a biological sense
the word was rarely mentioned;
among the faithful
jokes were clean,
intentions always honourable.

Once at the Prayer Meeting
a girl called Jane,
big boned and simple hearted
found everyone warming up
with a few exchanges of 'Knock, knock.'

She repeated a riddle
from the Works' canteen;
'What goes in dry,
comes out wet
and satisfies two people?'

The free air died in the room.
Bibles were examined for signs of wear,
coughs discovered.
Then Jane's child-innocent voice,
'A Tetley tea-bag.'

Laughter almost split the ceiling:
Jane's face shone like the moon.
Reverently she folded her hands to pray,
eager for the next instalment
of her love affair with God.

PRAYERS

You didn't subscribe to mornings,
left me to breakfast the children,
sort clean uniforms and books,
count their dinner money,
ferry them to school on my way to work.

The back bumper of my Escort
fell off in protest;
it couldn't stand
being slammed into the same tree
every day; we were always late.

You were praying,
would appear on the doorstep as we left,
your forehead printed with
three vertical lines from
helping God sort out the world.

I prayed also, fierce, frantic;
'God, how did I get into this?
For the children's sake
keep me going.
Don't let him find out about the gin.'

AT HOME WITH ANIMALS

The old tom let you submerge him
to get rid of fleas;
he'd been wanting to live in for weeks,
knew he'd won by your kind hands.
We sat on the rug with him afterwards,
picking off survivors.

You were reluctant to evict
the holiday cottage toad;
Flip Flop hopped on the linoleum
after we'd climbed into bed;
'I know you live here
but my wife would prefer you to leave.'

You brought home numerous hedgehogs
rescued from the road,
but drowned a mouse once,
tempting it with cheese
onto a plank of paper over water;
it leapt and splashed,

a slow death, terrified.
After that I caught them myself
in a jam jar, took the children
to watch me free them
in the graveyard.
You could be cruel sometimes.

I'LL TELL 'EE A TALE
'for John'

Rain on the caravan roof
nails us in for the morning.
What to do? We're bored with 'I Spy',
dominoes, comics, Simon and Garfunkel.
'I'll tell 'ee a tale!' Eldest son
becomes a Bristol sea captain,
entertains us with storm stories,
ghosts and other unlikely happenings.

When the sun comes out he and his sister
row the big broad-bottomed boat
on the sea loch, take apples and chocolate.
Later she returns alone.
'He wanted to fish, wouldn't let me stay.'
Waves worry the stones at the shore;
no sign of him. Not for an hour, two hours,
when he returns white-faced, having been
towed from the Atlantic tide by a prawn boat.
He's too hoarse to do justice to the tale.

WATER SPORTS

Too innocent the lap lap lapping
of water at little boats,
(I don't swim well),
but you persuaded me
to try the canoe.

Nested single on the water
I slid among reeds and lilies
on upland lochans,
paddled the sea loch
over graceful amber gardens.

There was an island of white sand
below small hills, Ristol,
where a family of horned, bearded goats
shifted their hooves
on lichen yellow rock at my approach.

Once a flotilla of ducklings
mistook my boat for mother,
changed clockwork gear in unison
to follow my wake
across the wind-blown water.

Sunset was best. I loved
to chase brittle darts of water shine,
would try to keep my craft true
along paths of Tennyson trembled light,
until the dark came down.

Sometimes I sailed with you,
remember the whale of Ullapool
huge and astonishing
which rose between us and the land,
cascaded in sunny water splash.

We watched seabirds,
aristocrats of inaccessible rocks.
But most times I let the children
share your dinghy.
I never really cared to crew for you.

HEARTBREAK HOTEL

The day that Elvis died
I was sitting under clear sun
in a Scottish Highland garden
full of cameo flowers.

Nextdoor's croft had hung hay
across the fence like washing;
its sweet scent drifted
over the books I'd brought to read,
the crackly radio.

A brittle voice from far away
broke the news.
I wasn't exactly a fan,
could never take seriously
those throbbing knees and tonsils.

It was the name carried me
to my father's raspberry scented garden,
June sun shining
on a day before I'd met
even the thought of marriage.

In a deckchair over the hedge
lounged a tanned young stranger.
He had the window open,
played 'Heartbreak Hotel'
that whole long summer afternoon.

Tiny yellow flowers wreathed my radio.
Elvis had ceased to feel lonely
and was dead.
I grieved for my girlhood,
distant bronzed young men,
my father picking raspberries in our garden.

FORMAL GARDENS

I was greedy for roses
during my fallow years,
used to visit formal gardens
where anonymous gardeners
kept wicked weeds at bay.

I liked to touch roses,
even now can scarcely bear
the frisson of
a white November bloom
cool in half light.

Winter was difficult.
How to get through
those cheerless,
flowerless months
with only cares for company?

I took a blanket,
bought numerous silks and wools,
sewed flowers
in the grey spaces,
each one a new blossoming.

Blending the colours,
learning the patterns
I became a creator of roses,
stitched them into my imagination,
threads to lure me
towards another, brighter spring.

REFLECTIONS

'The windows swivel round
so you can clean both sides.'
This didn't interest me.
I hosed them from the garden tap
when you were at work.

But there was still inside
to be tackled. It took all day.
Polishing, polishing
I saw my faded face in the glass;
when the sun went in
I disappeared completely.

MARBLE HALLS

No ceilings, no doors, a stepladder to the bedrooms.
Joan Sutherland's velvet voice echoed from the radio
round our new house; 'I dreamt I dwelt in marble halls.'
Wasn't I lucky, said friends, to have such a house
and such a clever husband to build it for me?
Comforts must wait. We had hot water and two taps,
a bathroom upstairs and plenty of space for furniture.
It would take time but I was promised nine sinks,
eleven rooms and an electric waste disposal unit.
I made up my mind to be pleased, swept grey dust
from room to room, cleared heaps of wood shavings,
fed corned beef hash and sliced loaves to the children,
took washing to the laundrette, tried not to complain.
But I felt bad. There was nowhere to rest in this maze.
Door spaces like question marks compelled attention;
pigeons woke me at dawn, hopping on the monopitch roof
above our bed. I longed for peace to read and write.

Of course things improved with time. We chose curtains,
installed a heating system, but it never felt like home.
I hated the land-locked kitchen, ruined batter puddings
weeping into the bowl after our rows. Which grew worse.
I welcomed news bulletins, invited swarms of visitors,
grew interested in the weather, anything to distract
from what I knew was happening to my marriage.
Our last November a tree blew down in the dark garden,
the ancient ash we'd used to name the house.
Hearing the crash I opened the door to touch twigs,
Great Birnam come to Dunsinane, death on the doorstep.
Next morning I rescued a slab of bark to take inside;
my family chopped up the rest. It wasn't difficult;
the tree was rotten, had been standing hollow for years.

NELLIE'S LITTLE PALACE

It was more like home than home,
each stick of furniture polished,
glass shining in firelight, cushions
waiting on a soft settee, warm teapot.
Auntie Nellie worked hard to keep it so.
She didn't have a job or children,
lived for love of Walter and their nest,
never kept him waiting for his tea,
organized her life to suit his clock.
Every Tuesday she caught the bus
at two, bringing sweets for my children,
left at four. I visited Saturdays
to share the box of Black Magic
he always bought her at weekends,
felt afraid when she talked of death;
'If Walter dies I'll die',
worrying over his angina pains.

In the end she was first to go;
dementia struck. Once when I came
she was calling from her bed,
welcoming phantom visitors.
The hospital could do nothing.
She grabbed our hands as we left;
'Go for a pass to get me out of here!'
As our backs turned her face
hardened with disgust at such desertion.
Death came soon, from pneumonia.
I'd gone to see her, found instead
Walter standing on the hospital steps
with her belongings in a plastic bag.
'She's dead' was all he said.
We drove home in silence
to draw the curtains, make tea
in the house she called her little palace.

FRESH START

Night air blew chilly round the sycamores,
but sap was rising; I could feel
promises growing in the peaty woods.

You wanted to surprise me,
switched the car headlights full on to reveal
a blaze of bluebells.

Hoodwinked into such an ardent show
the flowers yielded nothing
except their yeasty scent.
I wouldn't walk among them, stood instead
under the stars, reluctant to hold your hand.

RUMOURS

They say I married you
but I've denied it in the town.
It isn't certain to be true.

Because you're smiling in the street
they think
I have you at my feet.

Waiting by the library lift
your hand suckled mine
with an apple gift.

I've been seen after dark
with a man in a Humphrey Bogart mac
going into the park,

And someone claims a wedding
where the groom
left the bride's side
a distance too soon.

It isn't so.
Of course it isn't so.
We're different beings, you and I.
You with colours,
me with pen drew
separate worlds and never met again.

I tell the gossips this
when they insist I married you,
I tell them every day through tears.

I've been denying it for years.

ODI ET AMO

I wanted you
like lion skin
      to wrap
      my coward courage in.

I wanted you
to make it grow;
      you fed it poison
      sweet and slow.

Into each dream
the hemlock spread
      to plant a monster
      in my head.

Now every night
my fingers try
      to stop its breath,
      but it won't die.

TOP TIGER

             not one
      to take things lying down
      tiger in me
      hard asleep
      most times but when

then feel the lick
tiger tongue
        sweet Jesus
        things you've said
        a cold one hundred times

    why   won't   you   stop

    top tiger
whispers me fierce
     glow for it
     teeth   claws
          throat

but wait
gets you nowhere stoking tiger fire
                 stroke tiger fur

    make   him   lie   down

stop his breath
put out his eyes
take him apart
claw   by   claw

      feel the dead
      weight of him
      drag days down

      bite
      into your heart

ICE DREAMS

Night. All still.
Only my daughter in the next room
turns over and over
her unease about me.

Tears drenching my pillow
come as mist,
drift into my sleep.

The ice dreams come,
wandering grey ways
through silences of cold
where every night
I look for a cave,

and when I find it
see the dead child
curled at its mouth,
embryo corpse in a blue dress
frozen into the snow.

DRESSES

Clothes spoke to me in shops,
seduced my purse
with bold designer styles,
eye-catching colours.

New fabric smells,
the feel of silk or wool,
textures, blends,
hand crafting, bargain buys;
I was a professional spender,

hours
in fitting rooms,
slices of my salary.

Once an assistant forgot me.
I sat for a long time
in a strange frock
as the city dusk darkened
beyond a window,
watching the hushed mirror.
When she returned
I'd tired of the dress.

Snatched from their wardrobe
as I left
the dresses didn't like me any more.
Heaped on the back seat
of my getaway car,
limp, old-fashioned,
I felt their resentment speak
of times we might have had together,
carefree party nights
that never were.

RAPUNZEL

The sixties grew my hair to mermaid length,
dressed me like a princess with exotic taste.
Knives, I walked on, but such women I was for you!
French peach crêpe underwear, Italian shoes,
black velvet maxi, slit from hem to waist.

Russian in winter hat and trenchcoat;
'Tell Olga ve vill vait,' you used to tease;
Dutch girl in scarlet clogs, white lacy socks,
Indian temptress in a shi sha glass blouse;
Such women! Surely one of them would please

your eye, but one miserable day the witch
muffled me in a moon gold rainproof cape
lined midnight black, high leather boots to match,
shut me in her tower with only hair for company.
No escalator to the fashion floor. No escape.

At first you worked like double Jesus,
hacking the thorns that sprouted round the place,
used an armoury of weapons; I could hear the blows
of blunt machetes from my window, might have
helped by singing, but always the witch's face

would say 'No callers, no followers. You
are to live alone. It is your punishment.'
When you grew tired I cut my hair and escaped
through the roof, my petticoats hung on stars.
The witch found some other princess to torment.

I see her sometimes, stalking the streets
of our old marriage, looking for the warm café
that used to be there before the spell of her
enchantment. It's gone, but I like new places now;
clean corners fluorescently lit, artificial day.

LESSONS

Student 1966
was twenty two,
wore false front teeth and a wig.
She'd tried bosoms, she confided,
but found she looked deformed.

Her own hair,
neat and normal,
hid under a cape of flowing gold
adorned with emerald ribbons.

Her teaching was hopeful
but spasmodic; she explained
she couldn't work
if her love life wasn't going well.

Lunchtimes she ate a bag of salad
and read the serials
in Woman's Own;
she was a literature student.

One day she couldn't teach at all;
her love-life had eloped
with their joint bank account,
including a full term's grant.

The bank offered an overdraft;
with the money she bought ankle boots,
thick-soled and serviceable
but bright yellow.

'I stood them on the table
and just watched them all evening.'
Like many of us she found
the lessons of the sixties
took a long time to absorb.

SHALL WE GATHER AT THE RIVER?

1. My mother knew a parrot
    that could sing 'Glory for me'.
    She had the sense to leave behind
    the dubious sects of her upbringing,
    was shocked and shamed
    when I embraced one.
    Grandma Rose had clawed comfort
    from religion to lighten her world
    of imprisoning poverty.
    My parents believed in education,
    were proud of my Scholarship,
    spent good money on school uniform,
    had hopes for me.
    Now I was wasting my brains
    on Bible study and wanted to be
    a missionary. Why didn't I
    go dancing and enjoy myself?
    Didn't I realize I'd be young only once?
    Chains to chains in three generations!

2.   We sang gloriously at our church,
swelling brassières and braces
with Sankey favourites, choruses
from Alexander's hymnal;
'Showers of Blessing',
'Rescue the Perishing',
'Shall we Gather at the River?'
This last I liked best, still enjoy
the confident, striding tune,
words shimmering like a silver band;
bright angels, robes, crowns,
all the accoutrements of heaven
blended into one triumphant melody.
Soon we would see the Saviour's face,
know peace in the company of love,
acceptance all the happy golden day.

We swallowed the fraud
like urgent medication,
mouths wide open for the spoon,
a company of crippled spirits.
'Brother, Sister,
lay down your burden
at the shining river.
Bring your sickness,
the pain that's so hard to bear,
your grief over the loss of a loved one.
Bring that problem
eating at your innermost thoughts,
that unfulfilled ambition.
Bring your loneliness,
your aching heart;
bring them to the shining river.'

It seemed so simple.
The beautiful river.
I made the mistake of wading in too deep.
It nearly drowned me.

3.   One day when I arrived in church
I found my customary solitary pew
tied across with a pink ribbon.

It wasn't Christmas
or my birthday.

RESERVED

A large lying notice
lay on the seat where
nobody else ever sat;
(at the back,
too far from the preacher,
by the door,
draughty.)

I didn't hesitate.
This was Church where
I'd been going for years.
Its doctrine had reduced me
to a sweat of guilt and tears;
I had a right
to sit in my own place.

I cut the tape and sat.

Ridiculous, I know, to stay.
The world lived outside,
sun shone, trees were green;
I'd even come by car
for easy leaving.

More than ribbons
tied me to the place.
Under its expensive leaky roof
were twenty years of my life,
five thousand habit-forming hours.

Oh yes, I stayed,
stood when they stood,
wrapped my shawl tight round,
held my hymnbook high
but my mouth was empty.

I couldn't praise the Lord.

39

4. You are not from yourself
    but come from God
    to tell this woman to repent
    her sinful ways
    before it is too late.

    Straight fundamentalist stuff
    I once believed
    when a painful adolescence
    led me into the arms
    of loving Jesus.

    I married him and you,
    I know this,
    but half of love's grown cold.
    What's to be done?
    Stern choices stand at my elbow.

    I see a long green corridor of days
    with doors all closed,
    none of them labelled,
    no end to it, either.
    Where will it lead

    If I set foot alone
    along its distances?
    Which door to knock upon?
    No voice but yours and God's
    'This is the way, walk ye in it.'

    I'm deaf to both. This maggot
    feeds on the foundations
    of the trust we two
    once had in one another.
    It grows bigger every day.

5. On the Reverend's lounge carpet
    I wept like a waterfall
    and felt 'enough'
    bleed into my bones.
    Doubts became acceptances

    that I was no longer
    the doctrinaire believer
    of my youth;
    nor could I be a wife.
    That had to be faced.

    Long walks in the hills
    helped shape a new existence;
    the 'airy mountains'
    loved and feared from childhood
    became a fascination.

    I challenged them for space,
    set foot self-consciously at first
    on the crust of the earth,
    becoming braver
    with every mile of freedom.

    The tally of outdoor hours
    began to match the times
    endured at services;
    a new religion maybe?
    Strange if quiescent magma

    smoulders underneath
    each pebble of my life path.
    Which of us knows for sure?
    Hard to unlearn
    a lifetime's way of walking.

    I still dream
    dark Victorian churches.
    Daytime I live
    the weather of the high traveller,
    a few flowers, clear air.

    Breathing's become important to me now.

THE TREATMENT

The dentist was Evangelical,
Born Again, Reader
of Scripture Union Bible Notes.
Some one must have told I'd gone astray;
he waited until my mouth
was wedged open for the filling
then poured admonitions into my ear
about the Lord's forgiving ways.
His soft words drilled into my brain
like an SS interrogation.
Set free at last from his chair
I didn't wait to hear more
but paid on the spot, in cash,
eager to see the street again,
cultivated gardens, people, shops,
traffic, and most urgent of all,
the shelter of my own safe house.

TENDERLY

Wounds need open air sometimes
to help the flesh heal. When I peel back
the layers I grew to cope with loving
here's you exposed. The place feels sore.
Who did I kiss but you, under plane trees
in drizzly autumn, big leaves blessing us?
You brought books when I was ill,
blending our lives in printed pictures.
Was it my sickness tricked you
into thinking me docile, easy to subdue?
You were gentle with our firstborn;
I have your photograph, proud smile,
capable caring hands that became impatient
with trying to mould a family
to your designs as easily as wood or clay.
Wounds need air sometimes, to help them heal.
Here are mine. Touch them tenderly.

NINE LIVES
For my dear friends

Gillian taught me running,
cheeks and hair always healthy
with the joy of being free to move fast.

Twin Susans kept house, fridge full of food,
double oven humming, guests at the table,
cream where the cat couldn't get it.

Betty listened by the lake
to the wish of what the waves were playing,
Mozart's Clarinet Concerto.

Bertha cumbered about my rooms with such grace
she became shining Mary.
Flowers opened for her birthday.

Kate stored picnics in her life for children,
made safe their teddy bear woods
with laughter and jokes.

Joyce knew a thing or two, how to drive a car,
how to pack much into a little month,
how to reel the past into a bad B movie.

Barbara, sweet singer, put leaven
into the bread of city wanderings.
Dark eyes soon grow accustomed to the dusk.

These lives became the clapper of my stopped heart,
set its rusty weight swinging to meet new days,
ringing in the changes.

About the Author

IRENE RAWNSLEY is an ex-teacher who writes a great deal for children. Her first book of poems for young children
Ask a Silly Question was published by Methuen in 1988, and a sequel *Dog's Dinner* is now out from the same publisher. In September 1987 her poem-sequence *Hiding Out* was broadcast for schools. She takes her poems into schools and libraries as a visiting writer, and also works with teachers to promote the writing and reading of poetry in schools. Her poems for adults have appeared in a number of magazines and anthologies, and she was one of the prizewinners in the first Northern Poetry Competition, organized by Littlewood in the same year. She has been Membership Secretary of the Northern Association of Writers in Education since its inception, and lives near Settle in North Yorkshire.